CHRISTMAS JOY!

# Dedication

I write this book in dedication of the upcoming generations.

May you run mightily with the truthful story of Chrismas Joy.

Keep the torch shining brightly!

But the angel said to them, "Do not be afraid; for behold, I bring you good news of great joy which will be for all the people; for today in the city of David there has been born for you a Savior, who is Christ the Lord. This will be a sign for you: you will find a baby wrapped in cloths and lying in a manger."

Luke 2:10-12, NASB

# Contents

Cherish the people God brings into your life.

-- Nancy B. Velasco

## *Acknowledgement*

A very special thank you to my son Tito Blackmon Velasco and his girlfriend Kaitlyn Hughes who endured the early playing of many Christmas carols and worship songs way before December.  A special thanks to so many friends who kept reading my postings in social media  containing my thoughts on Christmas way before Thanksgiving even. Thank you to all the dear people at Celebration OC for their patience as I stayed home and worked at my kitchen table writing and formatting Christmas Joy! Most of all, I would like to honor and express adoration to my First Love who continually reminds me of Christmas Joy every single day of my life. Jesus! There would be no Christmas Joy without you!

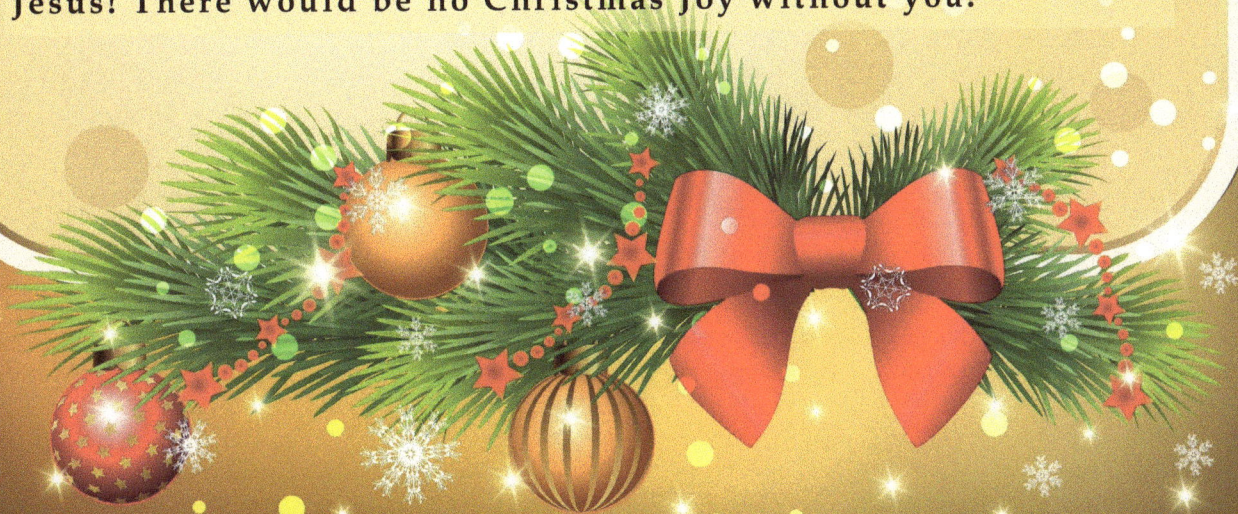

# Anticipation Lingers

*Therefore the Lord Himself will give you a sign:*
*Behold, a virgin will be with child and bear a son, and she will call His name Immanuel.*
*(Isaiah 7:14, NASB)*

Colorful wrapping paper, odd shaped boxes, ribbons and bows -- yes, there I sat amidst them all. My childhood memories include recalling the hours I spent there surrounded by unopened treasures, not just any treasures-- my treasures--the ones that held a tiny name tag bearing the word "Nancy" on them. Yes, I must admit to having shaken each one, and having felt through the packaging in an attempt to guess what each held inside. Would it hold a mere pair of winter socks, or a warm coat, or better, perhaps a prized party doll. You know the one -- the doll that would toss a ball with her plastic hands, or blow up a balloon if her mouth held the special blowing spout. Surely Momma would notice my desire for such a doll. Yes, suspense and anticipation would hang in the air as days seemed so long and Christmas so far away -- would it ever get here? Surely the treasures I circled in advertisement magazines or that I stared down as my mom and I went shopping --- these would end up in my closet or on my bed. Thoughtfully, and imagining victory, there I sat year after year digging through presents that were under the carefully decorated family Christmas tree.

Christmas holds excitement, anticipation, and much joy. Each year it seems hard to wait for that December 25th date to arrive. Expectancy fuels the bustling of seasonal activities and conversations. Even in today's society, people still eagerly await the coming of Christmas. People of all ages count down the days with hopefulness. Maybe you like me have gotten together with friends and made one of those count down chains, the ones that contained simple construction paper loops, one for each day. We would cut or tear off one loop each day until the chain no longer existed and Christmas had arrived. I imagine our anticipation of Christmas greatly pales in comparison to what it must have been like awaiting the arrival of the Messiah. After all, the arrival of Jesus, our Immanuel, took place many years after the initial prophecy that we read about in Isaiah 7:14. *"Therefore the Lord Himself will give you a sign: Behold, a virgin will be with child and bear a son, and she will call His name Immanuel (Isaiah 7:14, NASB)."*

Isaiah had announced the coming of Jesus way before Mary gave birth to this baby boy. This birth, the greatest in history, has the oldest baby shower invitation of all ages -- without doubt, God wanted to make sure everyone knew of the coming of Jesus. He wanted to invite everyone to a beautiful throne room of grace. This miraculous birth of Jesus by virgin Mary gave the whole world reason to worship with joy. This birth, highly anticipated for hundreds of years, brought with it the opportunity to get up close and personal with God and to establish an intimate relationship with our Creator, our Savior, and our First Love. It started here with the coming of Jesus!

I am sure all of heaven celebrated and looked on to witness God's glory, his very presence being sent in the form of a baby to earth. *"And the Word was made flesh, and dwelt among us, (and we beheld his glory, the glory as of the only begotten of the Father,) full of grace and truth. (John 1:14, NKJV)."* Wise men who studied the stars rejoiced (Matthew 2:10). In anticipation and with great joy, the wise men proceeded on their way to seek out this new king. Their anticipation turned in to worship as they presented the news of the then baby Jesus to people surrounding them in the village. The wise men had set out with provision, but also they came bearing gifts fit for a king. Obviously they knew the scrolls well and came with hearts filled with awe and joy. They bowed down before baby Jesus. They worshipped him knowing that their anticipation had come to fruition -- not just their anticipation alone, but that of the tribes of Israel.

I hope I never lose that sense of anticipation and awe in coming before our Lord. Oh, that I may come in anticipation each day in prayer and in fellowship with the Holy Spirit, my Helper! I am determined to wake up each day with an eagerness, and with a desire to spend time with God. Each day brings with it new joys and new hopes. What will the day hold as I ask the Holy Spirit to lead? Who will intersect my path? What divine appointments will God orchestrate? How will Kingdom seeds be sown? Who will come to know Jesus for the first time? What miracles, what manifestations of God's touch will I observe this day? Today, the day not yet lived out, holds great potential, promise, and hope when I walk with the King.

I hope you will find a new spark or flame inside of you, and that you will come with child-like faith in full anticipation. Experience the joy of Christmas again. Experience Immanuel -- "God with us". Experience Christmas Joy! The Joy that we spell J-E-S-U-S. Experience the daily joy of having a personal encounter and a personal daily walk with the Holy Spirit. The "Jesus" joy of Christmas can become a daily everlasting joy if properly embraced, received, and cherished. Right now, meditate on and grasp such treasure, such joy.

# Prayer of Anticipation

We give you praise. Lord, we love you. You are the most beautiful, the most loving, and we adore and honor you. May we constantly remember the joy of your birth. May we grasp the joy that has come because of your death and resurrection. Let us not just view Christmas Joy as a Christmas day kind of encounter. Let us go with hearts of joy every day because we walk with you Holy Spirit. Guide us, empower us, forgive us, and shine in and through us your amazing love, And let your joy burst forth in us to touch the world. Thank you for your truth and grace. Thank you for your amazing love. Heal every broken heart and every disease. Rekindle our love for you, our First Love. Let us have your heart beat and follow after you always.

# Keeping the Joy

*"But the angel said to them, 'Do not be afraid; for behold, I bring you good news of great joy which will be for all the people; for today in the city of David there has been born for you a Savior, who is Christ the Lord. This will be a sign for you: you will find a baby wrapped in cloths and lying in a manger.'*

*(Luke 2:10-12, NASB)."*

In some of the years gone by, for my friends and my family, the awaiting of Christmas held a different type of anticipation -- one of dread or even a bit of fear or apprehension. For me, most of these types of heavy anticipations stemmed from my own faulty mental processing --- thoughts that were burdened down: financial, relational, time allocation, etc. How can these kinds of thoughts come upon us and how can we still have Christmas joy?

Christmas, perhaps more than any other time of year, gets wrapped up with relationships and spending time with family, friends, co-workers, and those we know, or maybe those we are getting to know. In looking back over the years, some of the hardest Christmases were the ones in which for whatever reason someone I loved no longer could come for Christmas.

I still recall the first Christmas without my mom, cancer had taken her life. That first Christmas without her certainly panged my inner being, yet at the same time I felt deep joy as I recalled with fondest all the ways she had made Christmas special over the years. Now, when "O Holy Night" plays, I fondly remember her seated at the piano in our home, and me sitting next to her on the bench, and hearing her sing and play this beautiful song.

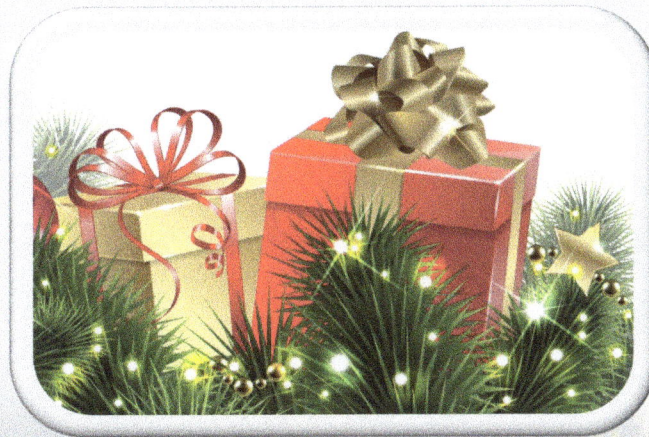

I recall her gentleness, her love, and her beautiful heart towards the babe of Christmas --- Jesus. I treasure that moment -- the moment of hearing "O Holy Night" and I treasure the Joy --- spelled "J-E-S-U-S." I believe her singing that song served as a seed to shape my inner views of Jesus, of God himself coming as a baby here to express his love towards us. When I really focus on it that way, though tears can still flow, I would not trade that special time for anything. I see it as a moment, but more so, I see it as "Christmas Joy".

The people closest to us, we do miss deeply. Yet this Christmas, I want to ask you a question, do you have any warm memories? Focus on all the Christmas planting instead of the people departing --- what got planted in your heart, in your mind. Even if the times were not necessarily as good for you -- it still helped shape what you value and treasure each day of your life. The moments shape what we value. Those are our precious moments of treasure that we keep as part of our being, we keep in our Christmas Joy.

Other happenings -- the ones worth erasing -- we choose to have removed by not dwelling there, not continuing to reflect there, and allowing God to heal those parts of our lives. Each of these still shape what we view as Christmas Joy. Allow these thoughts to birth joy rather than sadness. How will you shape Christmas this year? How will you influence those coming up after you -- the next generations? Who will you love on? With whom will you sing "O Holy Night"? Who will hear one more reading of the Christmas story? You, yes, you shape Christmas joy!

# Awaited Treasure
## By Nancy B. Velasco

Rushing feet, tiny shoes, heavy thuds along the path,
The rich, the poor, the loud, the quiet, shuffling
Towards a season filled with joy, hope, and peace.
At least that's what one might imagine if you please.

Oh, please no more sickness, and certainly we'd like no more
pain. Just hot chocolate, marshmallows or perhaps some honey
and tea, Something simple I would like for you my friend and for
me.

Think of snow covered mountains filled with snow covered trees,
Imagine icicles from house tops and shining stars in a midnight sky, and
Imagine ice scattered upon the seas.

Bundling up in throws in front of a gentle blazing fire,
Conversing with stories and laughing with glee,
Oh, if that were the picture of Christmas for you and for me!

Joyful Christmas carols, laughing with friends,
Roaming around in warm winter boots, adorned in thick woolen hoodies,
and leather slick gloves, we eagerly await that colder air, and fuss when
summer stays way too late.

Come on Christmas season we all seem to say.
Cozy beds, sweet dreams, apple cider scented air,
Oh that we might enjoy the Christmas season without a care.
Long, long, long ago,
Many, many, many years ago
People waited and waited and waited
Like a gift under the Christmas tree.

They waited for something special
Something very special indeed.
The most special treasure that
would ever come to earth,
The most precious, the most longed for,
The most priceless indeed.
All the coins in every bank
And all the gold on the earth
Could never, ever buy this beautiful
delight.

By now you must be wondering,
What could it be, this beautiful sparkling treasure
Better than anything,
Better than silver, better than gold,
What could hold such value and make everyone cheer?
What could those people of long ago long to see and long to hear?

A special baby came one night in a bustling little town,
It was wrapped not in a royal robe, nor did it wear a royal crown.
The baby came on Christmas day and laid amongst a pile of hay.
This little baby boy came full of love and full of joy.

This baby came to save the world from all the darkness that was hurled at it here. This baby came to show great love to everyone everywhere.

He came to show love to the rich and the poor, to the loud and the quiet, to the people far and people near. Such a babe we hold so dear.

This baby we know as Jesus,
Yes, God came to earth and wrapped himself up
as a tiny little baby and grew up to show he cared.
God came to earth as a tiny little baby.
He we celebrate on Christmas Day.

God came to earth as a tiny little baby.
He came to earth to save.
He came to save us from all the evil in the world,
From all the evil in our hearts.
He came to give us all a brand new start.

Joy much joy we proclaim on Christmas Day
Because of the one who came to save.
Joy much joy we proclaim because of Jesus,
This special babe who lay on that stack of hay.

# The Smells of Christmas

*"When He had taken the book, the four living creatures and the twenty-four elders fell down before the Lamb, each one holding a harp and golden bowls full of incense, which are the prayers of the saints (Revelations 5:8, NASB)."*

What scents do you think of when someone says "Christmas"? I think of all the smells coming from the kitchen. A special piping fresh hot bread smell fills the air as cornbread bakes in the oven. Cinnamon rolls, pumpkin pie, and apple cider all add a sweet aroma and tempt our appetites so much so that sampling deserts becomes most probable. The rising smell of a smoked turkey or honey glazed ham, barbecue brisket, or other fine meats, gradually takes over all the other scents and upstages the feast table as the main deal. Yes, I would say all of these aromas contribute and lead to the cries of "I'm hungry!" "Ready yet?" and "I'm starving!" I do not consider myself a gourmet cook in the kitchen; however, as long as I do not feel rushed, I enjoy baking pumpkin pie and other delicacies. Yes, certainly Christmas would not be complete without the wonderful smells that we have grown so accustomed.

In more recent years, around the holidays, I have gone to homes in which the preparing of cultural food adds not only a smell, but lends a tradition of community and friendship. Though the homemade tamales get scarfed down quickly once served, the steps and preparation involves an attention to detail while requiring planning and much time. Recipes get passed down to the next generation. Hopefully extra hands help to speed up the yielding of larger batches of delicious tamales. Tamales, enchiladas, home made lasagna, fried or rotisserie cooked turkey, and other special foods contribute to the feast of Christmas Joy. They also add to the creating of memories with friends and family.

In addition to the yummy food, setting out pumpkin scented candles also adds nicely to the scents of Christmas. Mingling, enjoying fellowship, and even times of being alone yet knowing people are going to be eating whatever I am preparing later adds to the Christmas Joy.

How many of us enjoy hot apple cider with perhaps a cinnamon stick or orange slices thrown into the mix? Winter time can get rather chilly, and maybe your home has a fireplace. Someone sets that up nicely to warm the room, or you travel somewhere that has a fireplace. I picture just sitting cozily near the fireplace with a small throw blanket over my legs, while sipping on a warm beverage such as hot apple cider. The season of setting up the fireplace, bringing out the throw blankets, preparing hot apple cider or even tea, and just enjoying time with family or friends adds to the warmth of Christmas Joy. The cozy environment comes alive, and the scents of the food and special Christmas season drinks dance in the air. Recipes, tradition, and culture get passed down from generation to generation.

Mostly, when I imagine the smells of the Christmas season, my mind quickly goes to pleasant smells. However, the real Christmas, the one in which Christ came as a baby, most likely did not carry with it such refined odors. More than likely the smell of animals and of people who had not had opportunity to properly bathed filled the air.

Joseph and Mary did not have reservations at a five star hotel in the city of Bethlehem.  Nor did they drive in an A/C equipped, praise rocking sports car to get there. *And she gave birth to her firstborn son; and she wrapped Him in cloths, and laid Him in a manger, because there was no room for them in the inn (Luke 2:7, NASB).*

My own sense of Christmas needs an adjustment as I remember the accustomed smells of baking in the kitchen. Should I not take into account the less pleasant smells, the ones more likely for Joseph, Mary, and even baby Jesus to have encounter, and tie those in with my memories of Christmas? Even if you have not personally lived in a rural place in which farm animals roam, I am sure you have visited a zoo or animal park. However, even in the animal parks and zoos, workers there often have the job of keeping things clean -- daily sweeping up the dung and hosing down the areas.

I recall at one of my early teenage year jobs I had a chance to make some extra money by working the second shift and lending a hand in the petting zoo of an amusement park. I thought this would actually be nice to be around the animals and small children and enjoy petting the little lambs, etc. Certainly the job held some of these tasks, but being the "extra hand" called on scene, I quickly got handed a small broom and dustpan. I got assigned to cleaning up the droppings of these animals.

Needless to say, my paradigm quickly changed -- I no longer took such delight in working in the petting zoo. Adding the Texas heat to the mix made the smell worse and even attracted flies at times.

I do not read of anybody being assigned to clean up after the animals in Joseph and Mary's day, so my mind imagines that these animals around them did poop and did make it smell.

Lest you think the animals of the day held the only biblical smell associated with Christmas, let me reassure you otherwise. The magi brought gifts to Jesus. *"After coming into the house they saw the Child with Mary His mother; and they fell to the ground and worshiped Him. Then, opening their treasures, they presented to Him gifts of gold, frankincense, and myrrh (Matthew 2:11, NASB)."*

Frankincense and myrrh were trees found noted in Bible times (Song of Solomon 4:14). On investigation, we find that myrrh got used as an ingredient in anointing oil and frankincense became an ingredient used in incense (Exodus 30:22,34). You can read all about the use of anointing oil in the Old Testament and in the New Testament. Anointing oil today represents the Holy Spirit being welcomed into every part of our lives -- especially for healing and for the manifestation of the miraculous.

Incense, a sweet aroma filling the air, the Bible associate this with our prayers. God sees our prayers as sweet aroma going up to him.

*"When He had taken the book, the four living creatures and the twenty-four elders fell down before the Lamb, each one holding a harp and golden bowls full of incense, which are the prayers of the saints (Revelations 5:8, NASB)."*

Though the Bible really does not expound on the intent of heart behind the gifts that the magi brought to Jesus, I believe that the giving of frankincense may have been their way of welcoming Jesus and acknowledging his deity status -- in essence I believe they were in reality expressing "Welcome Holy Spirit -- Welcome God!" Their actions added to this in that they bowed down and worshipped Jesus. When we enter into relationship with God, just like a relationship in the natural world, communication becomes key. The presenting of incense, which represents our prayers, I believe symbolized the entering into such communion or relationship through prayer. When we pray we enter into a rich relationship with our Lord.

As expressed already, Christmas joy, part of our lifestyle, means that anointed worship and prayerful adoration of our Lord become a daily encounter -- part of our journey with our Savior.

Let's backtrack, the smells of Christmas varies greatly. Our minds and noses recall the scents of the kitchen baking and candles that carry the scents so familiarly found in the Christmas season. Jesus though, along with Joseph and Mary, went through unpleasant smells associated with making their temporary home and birthing location in the manger -- they endured the smells associated with common livestock. The magi; however, brought on site the aroma fitting for our King Jesus -- anointing oil and incense ingredients.

I pray that this Christmas season and every day of your life and every day of my life we will welcome the presence of the Holy Spirit and come with hearts of adoration and worship.

## Christmas Scents

From pumpkin spice to dung filled animal caves,
From cinnamon rich to the smell of sin and shame,
Christmas scents we recall just the same.

The greatest scent of all is not that of the Christmas tree,
The greatest scent of all is the one of You dying for me.
Sweet Holy Spirit, fragrantly we welcome Thee.

Let our prayers arise.
Let the aroma fill the air.
Let our sweet communion forever gather here.

Reach inside our hearts.
Pour your sweetness there,
Your amazing love and grace we share.

## Welcome Holy Spirit

Oh Lord, we welcome you! We welcome you into each day of our lives! We desires your presence, your anointing, and surrender to you fully. We delight in communing and meeting with you. May our prayers go before you as a sweet aroma. Holy Spirit meet with us and thank you for always making intercession.

As we remember the smells of Christmas, we come and acknowledge that you endured the smell where your manger resided. You endured also the smell of our sin. Thank you for taking on our sin and dying in our place. May our very lives serve as a fragrant offering Lord.

We desire to walk with you daily. We desire to meet you in the intimate place of your inner chamber. We are your temple. We are your bride. We adore you and worship you. Thank you Lord for meeting with us and going with us 24 hours a day, 7 days a week.

Forgive us for those times that we get our hearts and minds and eyes off of you and seek to carry on without you. Lord draw us back to that place of intimacy with you. Let our lives be a beacon to the rest of the world as you dwell richly in us. In the name of Jesus we pray.

Amen

# Get Togethers

*"And suddenly there appeared with the angel a multitude of the heavenly host praising God and saying, And on earth peace among men (Luke 2:13, NASB)."*

When my heart thinks of beautiful Christmases of years gone by and also beautiful Christmases to come, I cannot help but think of all the wonderful people that helped in creating such memories. After all what would a Christmas potluck look like without all the various folk pitching in their fine specialties and delicacies. The stories, the laughter, the games, even the teasing, the caroling and fellowship --- these memories of Christmas mean gathering together to celebrate.

I know preparing for get togethers often take hours of thought and coordination. Even the preparation of food and ideas for what to do when everyone arrives takes time and commitment. If I invite people over, then time in cleaning and perhaps decorating and cooking come to mind. Yet overall the prep time and challenges end up with great returns on such investments. People investments yield greater returns than placing money in the stock market or purchasing a "thing" in an earthly sense.

God made the greatest investment of all. He holds the best parties as well. *"And suddenly there appeared with the angel a multitude of the heavenly host praising God and saying, And on earth peace among men (Luke 2:13, NASB)."* We could pass by this little Christmas verse and totally miss the most beautiful get together of the season. Heaven celebrated the coming of Jesus to earth. The Bible does not just say one angel came and expressed praise, rather, *"a multitude of heavenly host"* gathered together. I believe if I had been one of those shepherds tending to the sheep, this get together really would have freaked me out.   How many were in a multitude? We find clues of that in other parts of the New Testament.

Jesus would often share and talk to the multitudes. The feeding of the five thousand we know of as the feeding of the multitude, the crowd. Given that the counting method of the day did not include women and children--who did come and participate, I have heard it said that quite possibly this feeding of the five thousand actually consisted of twenty-five thousand or more people. I want to help repaint in your mind the scene of the shepherds hearing the announcement of Jesus' birth. Maybe like me you have etched in your brain this picture of a Christmas play in which a handful of kids or maybe a few adults play the role of the shepherds and then a few angel characters linger near among the sheep. Of course if everyone that came to participate in the play got assigned the role of these angels, we would have no more people to play the other roles.

Imagine this! If a multitude of twenty-five thousand of the heavenly host appeared to the shepherds during this birth announcement, that would be comparable to each angel taking a seat and occupying over half of the seats in the Angel Stadium in Anaheim, California. Yes, this get together happened like no other! Heaven hugely celebrated baby Jesus! From his birth Jesus did have quite an audience. Heavenly hosts celebrated him, and during his adult years people flocked to him. I picture him being really sought after by the people of his day. They sought to get together with this most amazing man -- the most amazing and only God. Most likely you know the stories of Jesus and his twelve disciples and how the people would gather around them.

Jesus did get away by himself to pray and to rest. However, the Bible makes it very clear that he had compassion for the people, for the crowds, and for those pressing in on him. He fed them spiritually, and at times even physically as we see in the feeding of the five thousand (and more). *"The people saw them going, and many recognized them and ran there together on foot from all the cities, and got there ahead of them. When Jesus went ashore, He saw a large crowd, and He felt compassion for them because they were like sheep without a shepherd; and He began to teach them many things (Mark 6:33-34, NKJV)."*

We come together to grow, and we come together also to have fun and enjoy each other's company. We come together as family and as friends. Christmas brings with it that time of year of coming together and also remembering the get-togethers that have already occurred in years gone by. I think coming together really does represent what God wants for us as we celebrate Christmas.

The enemy, powers of darkness, would want nothing less than to provoke separation, discord, disunity, and to lessen or dampen the otherwise overflow of joy that comes about when we gather together. When we come together as brothers and sisters in Christ with great unity, there God's presence comes in mightily. It not only comes with a glory cloud of thickness, things take place in the Spirit -- we see great power in the unity of the Bride of Christ. *"Truly I say to you, whatever you bind on earth shall have been bound in heaven; and whatever you loose on earth shall have been loosed in heaven. 'Again I say to you, that if two of you agree on earth about anything that they may ask, it shall be done for them by My Father who is in heaven. For where two or three have gathered together in My name, I am there in their midst (Matthew 18:18-20, NKJV)."* No wonder why we hear of so much spiritual warfare coming into a season called Christmas. The devil's purpose is to steal, kill, and destroy (John 10:10). Destruction often accompanies a spirit of disunity. News of suicide and depression get reported during this season.

Only as we push back and destroy the plans of darkness, and only as we lean into unity in Christ Jesus--as we meet together, do we find the veil of separation lifting. Come out of your cave this Christmas season, and put on the joy of the Lord as your strength and shield. *"Then he said to them, "Go, eat of the fat, drink of the sweet, and send portions to him who has nothing prepared; for this day is holy to our Lord. Do not be grieved, for the joy of the Lord is your strength (Nehemiah 8:10, NASB).'"* Do not succumb to the schemes and lies of the enemy (2 Peter 2:20). Rather walk in the light. Walk in love. Put aside anger. Put aside the spirit of offense. We forgive as God has forgiven us (Ephesians 4:31).

This baby Jesus, born in a city that was too crowded at the time to find proper lodging for him -- born into the crowded zone -- ministered and welcomed the people. He set the standard, the model for us. I know for me personally that really does become a model. For those who know me best understand that if I am in a very reflective and analytical mindset and working on things, I can start feeling rather uncomfortable if suddenly several people come in to where I am at. Yet, other times, I find myself craving company and may even start calling up friends and suggesting we go do something together.

Jesus did have compassion for the crowds, yet he too would break away for some alone time. He too would even safeguard his disciples from the mob of people and encourage them to gather as a smaller inner circle to fellowship together and to also teach them and impart to them. *"The apostles gathered together with Jesus; and they reported to Him all that they had done and taught. And He said to them, 'Come away by yourselves to a secluded place and rest a while'" (For there were many people coming and going, and they did not even have time to eat.) They went away in the boat to a secluded place by themselves (Mark 6:30-32, NKJV)."* We do gain much from being together as the Body of Christ, as the Bride, as the church. However, often we find ourselves getting to know a smaller group of people more intimately.

I believe that God places the inner circle of friends, mentors, and leaders in our lives to help us grow more distinctly. God places us together to speak into each others lives, to pray and intercede for one another, and to encourage each other. We encourage one another much like a pile of logs brought tightly together to form a fire. One log by itself may not burn as intently or as long in duration as a camp fire in which several logs are brought together. When we form tight knit togetherness in the spirit, this becomes breeding ground for the kindling of the fire of the Holy Spirit. *"For this reason I remind you to fan into flame the gift of God, which is in you through the laying on of my hands, for God gave us a spirit not of fear but of power and love and self-control (2 Timothy 1:6-7, ESV)."*

# When we Get Together This Year

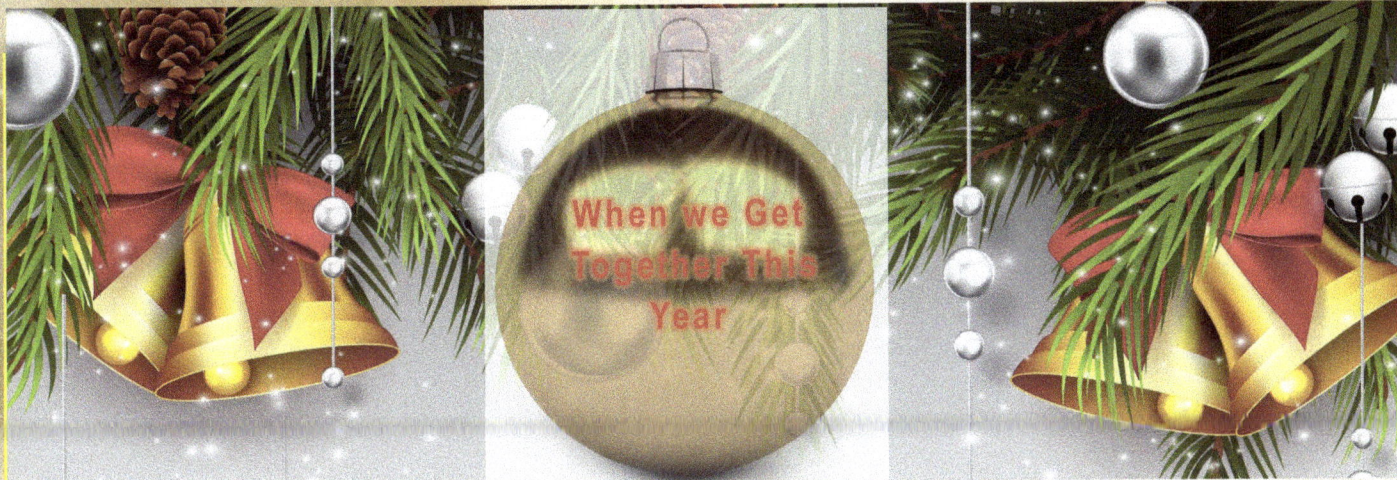

When we get together this year,
Lord help us not to fear.
When we get together this year,
Lord help us to have good cheer.
We celebrate your amazing birth!
We celebrate your amazing grace and
your coming here to earth.

As we sweep and prepare,
As we shuffle unaware,
Awaken our hearts to your
Abundant love,

Awaken our minds and wrap them in
Kindness like a glove.
No more fretting, no more shame.
No more arguing, no more blame.

Let forgiveness and gratefulness
Spring forth in us.
Let graciousness and unity
Overflow from above.

Yes, it's true we need
Your love every day.
Thank You for teaching us
And molding us today.
Let Christmas be special.
Be honored here we pray.

## Christmas Prayer of Joy

Lord,

We thank you for coming as a baby.

All heaven rejoices. We too rejoice.

Help us not to miss the joy of Christmas this year.

For those who journey, give them safety.

For those who grieve, give them comfort.

For those who feel alone, give them good friends.

For all of us, unite us in your amazing love.

In the beautiful name of Jesus we pray.

Amen.

# Shopping Spree

"Now in those days a decree went out from Caesar Augustus, that a census be taken of all the inhabited earth.  This was the first census taken while Quirinius was governor of Syria.  And everyone was on his way to register for the census, each to his own city."

Luke 2:1-3, NASB

Living in California, in certain areas, traffic can get very congested, which speaks to the fact that many people reside here. I also often find myself driving down the street that runs next to a popular shopping mall. During the Christmas season this particular mall gets very packed. In fact, though normally I might enjoy shopping there, I definitely avoid going in the mall and even take detours rather than drive on that particular street during the Christmas season. It gets absolutely packed in that area of our city, and the parking lots at the mall get fiercely packed with all the gift shoppers fighting over spots. The streets get jammed intermittently and waiting at the traffic lights at times takes several minutes due to the long line of cars also waiting for the light to turn green. Obviously the demand for shopping and going to the mall increases during this season.

Gift giving has slipped into our culture and has captured the hearts of many. Sales, shopping sprees, colorful advertisements, and even organized listings and reminder notifications of important birthdays and anniversaries have become tools of connectivity and used to remind us of friendships. Obviously this activity of gift giving has also prompted many a business to help us be reminded so that we just might by chance find a compelling reason to purchase their merchandise or obtain their services. The Christmas season, more than even birthdays, highly holds shopping and gift giving as key components. Through it all do we realize the most treasured gift -- Jesus?

Joseph and Mary found themselves in Bethlehem during the time of the census. I have a hard time getting my mind to grasp the full impact and weight of this particular census and the overall timing in which it took place. All places of the earth in which people lived got impacted. Caesar Augustus must have had a great deal of authority in order to demand that the entire population of the world adhere to the census. In any case, crowded with all the families of those originally born there, Bethlehem's inn had no room for Jesus. The Bible briefly paints a picture of that first Christmas town as having a great deal of congestion in it. However, Joseph and Mary did not go to Bethlehem to shop for a gift, rather Bethlehem became the place in which they birthed the most amazing Gift -- Jesus. Jesus became the Christmas Joy in our lives -- sent as the most treasured gift of all.

Having grown to adulthood, Jesus frequently journeyed with his disciples. We find in the Bible the story of Jesus stopping by a well to rest. I believe him resting by the well did not happen coincidentally. No, he ended up at that well for a special divine appointment -- the meeting with this woman who came out to draw water. She came to the well to meet a physical need. Jesus came to meet her at that same well to fulfill something deeper -- the spiritual thirst of her inner being. Jesus identified himself as the gift of God. He identified himself as the supplier of living water. "Jesus answered and said to her, 'If you knew the gift of God, and who it is who says to you, 'Give Me a drink,' you would have asked Him, and He would have given you living water.' (John 4:10, NKJV)."

The disciples would certainly have been right at home in our culture today. They met Jesus at the well and brought back food. I can just see them coming back from shopping in the city for food and having that satisfaction of having found delicacies or at least sustenance. Finding Jesus at the well with this Samaritan woman really sparked indignation in them. *"And at this point His disciples came, and they marveled that He talked with a woman; yet no one said, 'What do You seek?' or, 'Why are You talking with her?' (John 4:27, NKJV)."* The disciples came back ready to take care of Jesus and thought they would satisfy his physical hunger. They also became concerned perhaps of his reputation. Maybe they thought, "We have better things to do Jesus!" Let's get on to business as usual. Yet, Jesus' came as a beautiful gift into this woman's life. He does the same right now with you and me. He became a precious gift for all who would receive him. Back to Christmas! Stay tuned for the growing up of this little baby boy. Stay tuned for Easter!

Without the coming of a little baby, there would not have been a man dying on the cross to save an imperfect world from all the mess, all the "sin" throughout the ages. His coming to earth --- God clothed in flesh as a little infant in a manger in this congested city of Bethlehem -- marked a remarkable revealing of the most incredible gift throughout all history and throughout all time and throughout all the universe.

This special gift baby did not come on scene in a king's palace. Mary gave birth to Jesus and placed him in a manger. As I have listened to people describe the history and conditions of the birth of Jesus, some say that most likely the makeup of the place Mary and Joseph stayed looked more like a cave and that the manger that we place on Christmas cards resembled a feeding trough for the animals.

This place housed the animals and their food. This treasured baby -- God coming as man -- humbled himself in his birth and in his death. I have attended many a Christmas play that depict the place of Jesus birth as a neatly swept little abode -- it plays well; however, more likely the place of birth carried with it unclean and smelly animal droppings and darkness in a cold damp cave like dwelling. Jesus got low. He came humbly to reach out to us wherever we find ourselves. He came to reach out to us in our messes, in our imperfections, and in our hunger and thirst for more.

Jesus got low!  He got humbled. Why did he do so? Why did he come that way? I believe He came to lift us up and bring in the Christmas Joy -- new life in him.  You see, while Christmas does have that busyness to it and all the shopping, it also has emotions and life crisis with it.  Fights break out in shopping malls. People trampling one another to get that "entitled" item that has the lowest sale price. I believe as a society we have mastered putting up a front of everything being great at Christmas --  Jesus came so that we can openly go to God, we can meet with him, our Wonderful Counselor. Jesus came as Immanuel, God with us. "'Therefore the Lord Himself will give you a sign: Behold, the virgin shall conceive and bear a Son, and shall call His name Immanuel (Isaiah 7:14, NKJV).'" Yes, giving gifts certainly has expressions of love and we need to cultivate that special kind of shopping and giving of these presents. What a joy to receive a thoughtful present from a friend or  family member.  The giver took time to select it, to maybe even beautifully wrap it. I hope we give with this kind of heart. I hope we shop for gifts with that kind of desire.

In all our shopping and giving, let's remind ourselves and remind each other that the very, very best gift we can ever give anyone came wrapped up in swaddling cloths. *"If you then, being evil, know how to give good gifts to your children, how much more will your Father who is in heaven give what is good to those who ask Him (Matthew 7:11, NASB)!"* We are encouraged to ask of him. Just as a parents want the best for their kids, even more so does God want for us.

# A Very Special Gift

A very special gift,
Given to you and me,
A very special gift
Arrived for all to receive.

You cannot buy this gift,
Someone paid already you see.
You cannot give it,
It was already given when Jesus
Died for you and me.

This special gift,
Oh, such a bundle of Joy,
Came with tons of love.
Came from heaven above!

Jesus you are that gift,
Full of gentleness and grace.
Jesus you are that gift
who died in my place.

Now I go on a special shopping spree.
I go to find a treasure.
I shop and shop for hours it seems
And nothing seems to measure.

Nothing can measure up to the gift
You first gave me.
Nothing can measure up to the
treasure
I find in Thee.

-- Nancy B. Velasco

## Lord, It's a joy to celebrate!

We celebrate you Jesus! We give gifts to each other and remind ourselves of how much you have given to us.  You always give your best. Help us to always give our best too! Help us give our best especially to you. For everyone who goes on shopping sprees, I pray keep them safe. For my brothers and sisters, I pray especially that your fruit of the Spirit be evident in each of them.  Help us give as you gave and love as you have loved us.  As we shop with friends and family may special memories be created, sweet and neat. Allow your joy and your grace to show on every face. Forgive us for  times that we've grumbled or complained when things did not go our way. Forgive us for those times  we fought over parking spaces or over the last piece of whatever was on sale. Allow grace and mercy and forgiveness to go with us as we shop this year. Thank you for drawing us near to you. Thank you for being our treasure and our King. Thank you for your amazing grace. We love you Jesus! We love you our King! You are so special! We adore you! Your name be praised.

# Joyful Noise

*"And Joseph her husband, being a righteous man and not wanting to disgrace her, planned to send her away secretly. But when he had considered this, behold, an angel of the Lord appeared to him in a dream, saying, "Joseph, son of David, do not be afraid to take Mary as your wife; for the Child who has been conceived in her is of the Holy Spirit. She will bear a Son; and you shall call His name Jesus, for He will save His people from their sins (Matthew 1:19-21, NASB)."*

That's music to my ears! Yes, when we have been waiting on a medical diagnosis, or the results of a scholarly exam, or have been trying to solve a very difficult problem, and a solution arrives at last, we take great joy in hearing a positive report. A great sense of relief, accomplishment, and just sheer jubilance overtakes us. I can imagine the joy that Joseph must have felt when he learned that Mary did not cheat on him and that God even cared enough to send word to him to proceed with the wedding plans. We do not know a lot about Joseph's background and family, though we do know that he had already been in relationship deep enough with Mary to have committed to marrying her. It resonated as good news to his ears, a joyful noise so to speak, that his relationship thus far had not been in vain. Quite the contrary, they were selected to parent Jesus, the very Son of God. Also, the angel could have greeted him as "Joseph, the son of Jacob." We find though, the angel announced "Joseph, the son of David." This angel brought the joyful sound of the covenant promise. Joseph's identity got linked to the linage of honor that belonged to David, his well known forefather. What a joy to hear of such promise and such covenant expressed in this way!

We too can hear good news! We can hear the Holy Spirit and identify as God's children, as his kingdom family members. What a joyful noise or sound! We who once had no way of living for all eternity because of our sinful state -- after all we live in this dark world. Now instead of the bad news of hell as our destination, we hear the sound of our Lord reassuring us daily. We hear the Holy Spirit, our Helper guiding us very gently and mightily. Oh what a joyful noise! Hear this joyful noise ring clear and sure. Do you believe?

Do you receive the good news that Jesus died in your place? Jesus who lived here as perfect God, though also man in the flesh, went to that cross for you, and he rose again.

It says in the Bible that once you receive such good news, and turn from evil, turn from false thinking, and you should get baptized as instructed in Acts, and the Holy Spirit becomes your Helper. "Peter said to them, *"Repent, and each of you be baptized in the name of Jesus Christ for the forgiveness of your sins; and you will receive the gift of the Holy Spirit (Acts 2:38, NASB)."* What a joyful sound -- the sound in our hearts, the resounding inner assurance that the Holy Spirit dwells in you and me. What a joyful noise knowing that Jesus promised to go ahead of us and prepare a place just for us.

*"'Do not let your heart be troubled; believe in God, believe also in Me. In My Father's house are many dwelling places; if it were not so, I would have told you; for I go to prepare a place for you (John 14:1-2, NASB).'"*

You know in Joseph's mind he took a great deal of risk continuing in relationship with this pregnant woman. The risk in his mind diminished when the angel appeared in his dream and let him know he, Joseph, could continue shamelessly pouring in love into that relationship. No, he did not have to abandon ship. This marriage had purity and God's absolute favor on it. Joseph believed the report of the angel and the report of Mary. He had the honor of having such a beautiful bride and the honor of parenting Jesus.

"Shout joyfully to the Lord, all the earth; Break forth and sing for joy and sing praises. Sing praises to the Lord with the lyre, With the lyre and the sound of melody. With trumpets and the sound of the horn Shout joyfully before the King, the Lord
(Psalm 98:4-6, NASB)"

Our invitation to accept the birth of Jesus as real -- God clothed in flesh -- and to accept what he did on the cross for us as real, really paves the way for us to also have the honor of entering into a close relationship with God. Accepting this Christmas Joy invitation stands out as the most important and fulfilling decision you can ever make in your life.

*"For God so loved the world, that He gave His only begotten Son, that whoever believes in Him shall not perish, but have eternal life (John 3:16, NASB)."*

I believe the reason many people do not view the sounds of Christmas as joyful lies in the fact that they do not fully recognize Jesus. They have not comprehended the significance of his birth and that God chose to wrap himself in flesh as a baby. Certainly we see this as the case for the Samaritan woman in the Bible. Jesus, no longer a baby, had begun his ministry on earth, and he had walked among them for some time, yet the significance and truth of his identity did not fully catch on -- at least not for this lady. However, Jesus showed love and kindness and gave her opportunity to see and to know. She did not seem opposed to the sound of worship; however, she did not yet see Jesus as the one worthy of such adoration.

*"'But an hour is coming, and now is, when the true worshipers will worship the Father in spirit and truth; for such people the Father seeks to be His worshipers. God is spirit, and those who worship Him must worship in spirit and truth.' The woman said to Him, 'I know that Messiah is coming (He who is called Christ); when that One comes, He will declare all things to us.' Jesus said to her, 'I who speak to you am He (John 4:23-26, NASB).'"*

How often do we forget as we gather and sing songs of worship and praise and even Christmas carols. Do we fully grasp the presence of our King? Do we make a joyful noise or does it become more of a clanging cymbal void of love. *"If I speak with the tongues of men and of angels, but do not have love, I have become a noisy gong or a clanging cymbal (1 Corinthians 13:1, NASB)."* Oh what joy to reflect, to comprehend, to fully grasp, and know that this little baby born that Christmas morning brought hope, brought new life, and he brought the very presence of God himself.

Our response can reflect such good news, such goodness, and our voices can rise up in song and cheer. Our voices can resound with a joyful noise as we fully step into knowing the meaning of Christmas and embrace and worship our Lord and King Jesus.

Mary, pregnant with Jesus, prior to the manger scene and trip to Bethlehem made another journey. She visited Elizabeth, her relative. Elizabeth carried John the Baptist in her womb and Mary, as you know, bore Jesus. The Bible records that the baby in Elizabeth's womb leaped. *"For behold, when the sound of your greeting reached my ears, the baby leaped in my womb for joy (Luke 1:44, NASB)."* Mary and Elizabeth held a special bond of friendship and of divine calling. John the Baptist would grow up and announce the coming of Jesus at the beginning of his ministry. These ladies had joy because they carried joy. They carried the promise and got to see these two births come to past. What a joy for Mary to have been chosen to birth Jesus! What a joy for Elizabeth to have the assignment, the calling for birthing and raising up John the Baptist!

I enjoy hearing the song, "Joy to the World," that traditional song that gets sung, played, and orchestrated in so many ways year after year. I pray this Christmas season and all throughout the year, this special joy comes springing up from deep inside of you. Let the struggles of life be given over to God to help lead you through them. Embrace the joy, the magnificent joy of knowing Jesus and celebrating his coming. This same baby Jesus grew up and expressed it this way, *"Come to Me, all who are weary and heavy-laden, and I will give you rest (Matthew 11:28, NASB)."* This baby Jesus came to bring joy into your life. He came to bring his life into you. He came to allow you the opportunity to give him all those things that weigh you down. After all, the Jesus I know, still lives here as the Holy Spirit. Let the Wonderful Counselor walk with you.

*"For a child will be born to us, a son will be given to us;*
*And the government will rest on His shoulders; And His name will be called Wonderful Counselor,*
*Mighty God, Eternal Father, Prince of Peace (Isaiah 9:6, NASB)."*

# Joy Deep Within

Deep within and bubbling so,

Deep within and dancing aglow,

Holy Spirit burning in me,

Holy Spirit do they see?


Do they see the change in me?

Do they know who I use to be?

Do they see your hand at work?

Holy Spirit do they see?


You are my joy!

You are my King!

You are my love of which I sing!


Christmas joy for all eternity.

Joy! Joy! Joy inside of me!

# Burst Forth Prayer of Joy

Lord, we give you all those things that weigh us down.

We embrace the truth of your Word. You are God.

We come to you with any weariness that may be in us.

Allow Your joy to burst forth in us.

Allow us to walk with You daily.

Open our hearts, our eyes, and our ears to know You.

Lord Jesus we believe in You. You are the one that makes

things that look impossible, possible. We trust you truly.


In Jesus Name,

Amen.

# Star Bright

*"Now after Jesus was born in Bethlehem of Judea in the days of Herod the king, magi from the east arrived in Jerusalem, saying, 'Where is He who has been born King of the Jews? For we saw His star in the east and have come to worship Him (Matthew 2:1-2, NASB).'"*

Just a flashlight, yes, that plus some books that my grandmother gave me brought a new adventure into my life. I discovered that the flashlight would brighten an otherwise dark bedroom so I could continue reading. I would not have labeled me an avid reader or anything like that; these books came from my grandmother's house, so to the heart of a young girl, they held the world of adventure and worth the read. I did want to respect the bedtime ritual of turning off the lights, so those of course were off. My peach colored quilt became a tent of sorts as on top of my bouncy bed I would curl up under the covers, turn on my flashlight, and begin to read with excitement -- at least until I fell asleep, which often did not seem to take very long at all. Such a clever invention, the flashlight, wouldn't you agree? It can turn even the darkest of nights into a light filled arena. However, as clever and ingenious the invention of the flashlight, such artificial light pales in comparison of the true star light created by the God of the universe.

Skies filled with twinkling stars still bring out a sense of wonder and delight in me. I still remember the joy of seeing the sky dancing with the tiny sparkles. Just the dazzle of it all would inspire me to slow down and gaze upward.

Some nights a shooting star would even steal the show by quickly moving through the dark night sky. From our advantage point each star appears as a tiny dot dancing in the atmosphere, in actuality each spans across massive amounts of space and lights up for miles and miles. No wonder God chose a bright star to serve as a beacon to lead the magi to a place of worship at the feet of baby Jesus. This star lighting up the otherwise dark sky became the compass for their historical journey.

Could the star that led the way also have served as a reminder of the day? The Bible shares the covenant God made with Abraham. *"Then the angel of the Lord called to Abraham a second time from heaven, and said, 'By Myself I have sworn, declares the Lord, because you have done this thing and have not withheld your son, your only son, indeed I will greatly bless you, and I will greatly multiply your seed as the stars of the heavens and as the sand which is on the seashore; and your seed shall possess the gate of their enemies. In your seed all the nations of the earth shall be blessed, because you have obeyed My voice." So Abraham returned to his young men, and they arose and went together to Beersheba; and Abraham lived at Beersheba (Genesis 22:15-19, NASB)."*

Abraham, known as the forefather of the nations -- remember the Children of Israel? - - Abraham continued to go through testing of his faith. Initially he had no children, not even one. Sarah birth Isaac in their latter years. God tested Abraham's level of trust and obedience.  God led Abraham to go up to sacrifice his beautiful son Isaac -- his only son. Abraham chose to obey God and made the trip up the mountain with his son Isaac. God stopped Abraham and did not have him slaughter Isaac. More over, God commended Abraham's willingness to obey.

At this point of obedience we find God setting in the starry sky a visible manifestation or reminder of the covenant or promise made to Abraham. Every time Abraham looked up in the sky and saw all those stars, he got reminded that God had promised to bless him and multiply his seed. This promise, this covenant, got passed down generation after generation. Seeing a star covered sky would echo the covenant God had made to multiply the number of people descending from the lineage of the Children of Israel and also the promise of victory over their enemies.

Just like with Abraham, God still desires our obedience. He desires that "First Love" place in our hearts and lives. Jesus came not just so we could think of a cute baby in a manger. He came to make a way for not just the multiplication of physical lives -- more babies in essence. Jesus came for heavenly multiplication. Jesus came for more and more people to come into the grace fold of his amazing love for all eternity. Jesus came to welcome us into the Kingdom of God as God's royal family. No wonder the Bible records, *"Jesus said to him, 'I am the way, and the truth, and the life; no one comes to the Father but through Me (John 14:6, NASB).'"*

We find extended arms welcoming us. We find Jesus inviting us into an eternal relationship with him. That single star shown brightly and led the magi to the place of worshipping Jesus. Jesus has become our single source of coming into fellowship with God. No my friends, all roads do not lead to heaven. In fact, King Herod, on hearing from the magi and of their quest to find baby Jesus, brought in all the imitations -- the false hearted religious leaders of the day. King Herod sought to follow the words of men and his own ego than to fully grasp the full meaning of Christmas and to really understand that Immanuel, the Savior, Jesus was born (Matthew 2:1-12). He did not follow the star and worship Jesus, rather he order the execution of the baby population thought to contain the home in which Jesus stayed.

King Herod in a way thought that by murdering all the baby boys he could somehow stop God's plan. Despite God planting a star in the sky as a navigational compass, Herod, egotistically thought the bringing in of the Messiah came under his jurisdiction and power. Thus, Herod thought that he personally could stop the arrival of this God child, or at least murder Jesus before a royal throne could emerge.

That star, a historical marker, stood as a divine milestone in the sky. It noted God's promise, his covenant, and plan. Be encouraged and learn something from that star being positioned that way. God designs and places markers in our lives to show the way, to confirm and affirm his plan and his presence today. These often get overlooked, or called out as merely coincidental. The Bible, filled with truth, announces that God has prepared so much for us, and has a beautiful plan for each of us (Jeremiah 29:11).

The Holy Spirit, our Helper leads us daily and God gives us dreams, visions, and speaks to us through his still small voice. He also speaks to us through the Bible and through other people. I am coming to grips with the reality that much like that bright star that led the magi to baby Jesus, he daily shows the way in my life. He shows the way in your life too. The question becomes one of paying attention, giving heed, believing, and following after God. We being the figurative sheep in the Bible, hear the voice of the Holy Spirit and follow him.

*I am the good shepherd, and I know My own and My own know Me, even as the Father knows Me and I know the Father; and I lay down My life for the sheep. John 10:14-15, NASB*

## More Than a Star

You came so meekly into the world, so long, long ago.
You came shining God's love so brightly and clearly day after day.
Your shine was not found in a royal earthly throne or a head worn crown.
Your shine was not found in the riches of man.
Your shine was different and felt deep within.

Jesus you grew, and grew, a baby you would not remain.
For you became as a man, to live, to die, and to save.
You came to shine in a dark, cold world
You came to hurl the darkness away.

A way out of bleakness, and suffering, and pain.
A way filled with hope, with peace, and with love.
Jesus, you came!
Jesus, you came!

When my life has battles and storms as it sometimes will,
When my heart feels so heavy and bent over with grief,
Lord Jesus your light shines bright as that star in the night.

When everything seems to go all uphill,
When everything seems to go downhill too,
I know that you will see me through.

Your life is that light shining so brightly.
Your life you gave just for me.
You laid it down so that I might see.
You laid it all down to set me free.

# *Light the Way Prayer*

Dear Lord,

Thank you for leading the way each day. You really do hold the keys to all eternity. We lean not on the understandings of man. Rather we trust in you and in your love. We trust in the promises that Jesus, you bring. Surrendering to you happens every single day. We lay down all our idols at your feet. You alone came as God, Lord Jesus. You alone came also as man.

No other do I know who would die for me. No other one so compassion and meek would come to earth to show such care. Only my God. Only my Lord. Only the one true King. Help us not forget that you are right here Holy Spirit. Help us not miss the true meaning of Christmas. You are here!

In Jesus name.
Amen.

# Distant Lands

"Now in those days a decree went out from Caesar Augustus, that a census be taken of all the inhabited earth. This was the first census taken while Quirinius was governor of Syria. And everyone was on his way to register for the census, each to his own city. Joseph also went up from Galilee, from the city of Nazareth, to Judea, to the city of David which is called Bethlehem, because he was of the house and family of David, in order to register along with Mary, who was engaged to him, and was with child. While they were there, the days were completed for her to give birth. And she gave birth to her firstborn son; and she wrapped Him in cloths, and laid Him in a manger, because there was no room for them in the inn (Luke 2:1-7, NASB)."

The Christmas season brings with it thoughts of travel, bundling up, and going out to visit friends and family. I can still remember my parents taking time to drive us around to see Christmas lights. During my younger days it seemed so real! Dancing deers with Rudolph leading the way; snowmen dressed up in attires consisting of carrots, hats, and scarfs; and especially anything positioned way up high on top of rooftops that sparkled, flashed or changed colors fascinated me. As a youngster, it seemed as if we were driving and traveling to see those lights for hours on end. Now, I still enjoy seeing all the Christmas lights and driving around. However, back then, with such a child-like imagination, I enjoyed it even more.

My most delightful Christmas travel though involved going to my grandparents' house on Christmas day. It seemed like we would never get there. My brothers and I would fuss in the back seat of Daddy's Oldsmobile and try to occupy time playing little road games or hopefully falling asleep.

As burdensome as all the travel felt, the arrival and the time at my grandparents' made it all worth it. Our aunts, uncles, cousins, and grandparents would join in celebrating Christmas. Maybe you too have had some wonderful seasonal adventures.

Depending on the distance and length of stay, more attention ahead of time most likely fills your schedule. Such activities might include packing suitcases, preparing special travel snacks, planning itinerary, attending to safety preparedness and such before leaving, making arrangements to take time off from work, stopping the mail and stopping other services while away, and hiring a pet or house sitter.

In today's society our travel planning has grown complex. However, imagine what it must have been like for Joseph and Mary to travel to Bethlehem. No automobiles or airplanes, no air conditioned or heated travel, and no fast food spots lined the way. The ruling forces of the day demanded a census and as a result Joseph and Mary traveled to Bethlehem. This decree actually setup the fulfilling of prophecy -- a prophecy that had been declared years prior to such an amazing journey.

"'But as for Bethlehem Ephrathah, Too little to be among the clans of Judah, From you One will go forth for Me to be ruler in Israel. His goings forth are from long ago, From the days of eternity.' (Micah 5:2, NASB)." Christmas plays depict Mary and Joseph traveling quickly from one side of the stage to the other side of the stage to get from Nazareth to Bethlehem, the time duration for the play must finish and all applaud in time to go home in the same evening. In actuality, scholars believe that the distance between Nazareth and Bethlehem most likely comprised of approximately 80 miles. Joseph, a good man, sought to obey God and the officials of his day, and made the journey (See Luke 2:3-5). In the Christmas account, he faithfully submitted to the leadership placed over the land and obeyed.

This couple, Joseph and Mary, traveled back to their roots, but more importantly, in their obedience God blessed their linage by carrying out the covenant promise he himself had declared.

Joseph traveled the distance for the census as instructed. God favors our honoring of those that are placed in leadership over us. Each day we submit to leaders in our lives. Our submission and honoring of our leaders does not mean that we worship them, rather we respect their appointment into offices and authority. *"Obey your leaders and submit to them, for they keep watch over your souls as those who will give an account. Let them do this with joy and not with grief, for this would be unprofitable for you. (Hebrews 3:17, NASB)"* Jesus, the Son of God, came into the lineage of David during his birth in Bethlehem. Remember Joseph and Mary went to Bethlehem because of the census. They were required to go back to the town of their roots so to speak. Even this census and the associated travel provided a nice touch by further emphasizing the lineage lines of Jesus and tying them to David. Remember Bethlehem also became known as the "City of David".

God blesses us as we walk in obedience and journey with him daily -- we are led by the Holy Spirit. Our spiritual walk can in some ways be likened to traveling a distance in the natural or physical sense. In the spiritual sense, we find the concept of walking in obedience in the Bible as early as when the first king, King Saul, got appointed to lead the Children of Israel. Everyone traveled up the mountain to have a time of sacrificing together, and King Saul got impatient and perhaps fearful, and did not want to wait any longer for Samuel to arrive (1 Samuel 13). Samuel being of the Levite tribe should have been the one to offer the sacrifice. King Saul though acted presumptuously by taking matters into his own hands and as a quicker solution decided to "do it himself" -- he decided to offer the sacrifices to God on behalf of the people. Saul acted out of disobedience and did not pay honor to Samuel, the one chosen by God for this purpose as a spiritual leader, thus Saul in turn ended up showing dishonor to God. As a result, God conveyed to Samuel that the kingship would be torn out of the hand of King Saul.

We observe that favor got removed from Saul's life as a result of disobedience to God. Favor instead got placed upon David, the giant killer (1 Samuel 17:48-51). This same David also became so noted in the Bible as being the one after God's own heart. In response to King Saul's disobedience, the Bible notes, *"But now your kingdom shall not endure. The Lord has sought out for Himself a man after His own heart, and the Lord has appointed him as ruler over His people, because you have not kept what the Lord commanded you. (1 Samuel 13:14, NASB)."*

So, why do we talk about David or rather King David when speaking of Christmas Joy? We do so because of his relationship in the linage of Jesus. In the New Testament, Stephen, appointed as a deacon, while sharing thoughts regarding historical happenings involving King Saul and the new King David explained God's actions this way, *"After He had removed him, He raised up David to be their king, concerning whom He also testified and said. 'I have found David the son of Jesse, a man after My heart, who will do all My will.' From the descendants of this man, according to promise, God has brought to Israel a Savior, Jesus, (Acts 13:22-23)."* Over and over again, God blessed David because of his obedience and faithfulness. He was the one after God's heart because of his integrity, and became a prominent person in the family line.

We find "Distance" portrayed in two senses in the coming of the Messiah, Jesus. The journey to Bethlehem required traveling a distance and of course must have been very uncomfortable for Mary, pregnant with baby Jesus inside of her womb. However, given the time in which Mary lived and considering the penalty of conceiving outside of marriage, I wonder if those not really understanding kept Mary's friendship at a distance -- a personal alienation type of distance. I wonder if she got viewed as an outcast.

The seed inside of Mary had a supernatural origin; it did not come from Joseph. Mary, impregnated by the Holy Spirit must have had some interesting questions asked of her. After all, who would have thought God would work in this way? People viewing Mary as scandalous, and who did not understand God's divine knitting and work in her life must have also totally disregarded the holiness of Jesus and him being deity, being God. What seemed so far fetch actually did become reality. Isaiah prophesied years earlier that Jesus would be born of a virgin. God used all of this to lessen the distance felt between God and mankind.

Jesus arrived on scene
in such conditions -- some believed
and others did not.

"Therefore the Lord Himself will give you a sign:
Behold, a virgin will be with child and bear a son,
and she will call His name Immanuel
(Isaiah 7:14, NASB)."

God can relate very well to our struggles that we go through when people do not believe us all the way. Have you ever experience a time in which something extraordinary happened in your life or happened in the life of someone dear to you, and those around you had a hard time believing your testimony, or believing your story? They had a hard time believing that something like that would truthfully happen?

Despite the prophecy written down years earlier in Isaiah--written by someone that did not even live during the lifetime of Joseph and Mary-- despite the facts recorded matching exactly to the Christmas account -- the birth of Jesus -- many people have chosen not to believe. As incredible as it does sound, God did come to earth in the form of a baby. The man we know as Jesus walked on earth as both man and God. What a precious baby that came to life in that distant town of Bethlehem. However, in actuality the Spirit of God has no beginning and no end. So in essence Jesus already existed before being clothed in flesh. Oh, if we could only grasp the implication of it all. Our eyes would open up to see God's really amazing love for you and for me! What a beautiful and joyful Christmas!

Far away in Bethlehem, the little baby laid, far away in Bethlehem this God child wrapped in cloth laid in a manger on a pile of hay.

Bethlehem, Oh people living there,
Do you know the prophecy,
Do you even care?

A babe will be born by a virgin you see,
No ordinary child will this One be.

Rise up! Rise up!
Greet this One, chosen as King.
Rise up! Raise your banner and
Give Him gifts and sing.
Bethlehem, Oh Bethlehem the census
did take place. Let all history record
this birth of Jesus and His saving grace.

## A Prayer of Closeness

Lord Jesus you went the distance in coming here to earth.

You continually go the distance for us every day.

You do so to bring us close to you.

Lord, we pray for all who are feeling at a distance right now.

Help them feel your love.

Wipe away the tears of loneliness., grief, and pain.

Thank you for drawing us closer right now.

Increase our awareness of your presence.

Protect those who travel this season and keep everyone safe.

May their travels be filled with joy and the making of special memories. Lord you invite us to draw near to you and to go with you each day.   Let there never be a day in which we feel far away from you.

Forgive our sins Lord and draw us back to you.

In Jesus name,

Amen.

# CHRISTMAS BABY

*"While they were there, the days were completed for her to give birth. And she gave birth to her firstborn son; and she wrapped Him in cloths, and laid Him in a manger, because there was no room for them in the inn (Luke 2:6-7)."*

In today's modern scientific baby birthing medical facilities, OBGyn's share with the new parents to be their "delivery zone". No one is ever really ready though! Based on a variety of factors and variables, the doctors often forecast and provide a window of calendar time in which a newborn might arrive. Are you or someone you know currently expecting? If so, you might take on the approach I chose as I awaited the birth of my son. I decided that printing out a calendar sheet and brightly highlighting the delivery zone dates, and then magnetizing the calendar onto the refrigerator door made it obvious when this little one would arrive.

The delivery zone equates to the expected dates in which the mom might possibly go into labor, the birth pains commence, and the delivery and birthing pursue. Unless the couple chooses a scheduled C-Section or another method of timing the birthing process, the actual coming on of the laboring and birthing does hold some level of mystery. Due to not knowing when the baby will be born, part of the preparation for a newborn's arrival often includes the arranging and packing of a suitcase in advance of the actual day for rushing to the hospital or other birthing facility. Inadvertently, the labor pains arrive at odd times and the couple, ready or not, begin the process of welcoming a new addition to their family.

*"Then the king of Egypt spoke to the Hebrew midwives, one of whom was named Shiphrah and the other was named Puah; and he said, "When you are helping the Hebrew women to give birth and see them upon the birthstool, if it is a son, then you shall put him to death; but if it is a daughter, then she shall live (Exodus 1:15-16, NASB)."*

Before we jump into the birthing of Jesus, I want to journey back to the Old Testament to the birth of Moses and look at some similarities. You may know this Bible story, Moses, as a baby, could have been murdered. His living seemed rather impossible; however, look at all the ways God provided for his safety. Pharoah had order the execution of all newborns in an attempt to kill off future competition and opponents. The midwives were convicted not to allow the baby to die. The mom prepared a water resistant basket that baby Moses got placed in before putting both him and the basket into the water. Next, Pharaoh's daughter just happened to go for her bathing at that same bank of the Nile in which the baby's wicker basket floated. Moses' sister spied the scene nearby to observe his fate. The sister became instrumental in Pharaoh's daughter requesting and unbeknownst to her having the baby's own mother fetched for the purpose of rearing this boy. I do not think for a moment that these events or happenings took place by chance or coincidence. God orchestrated the safety of the man that he had already chosen to lead the Children of Israel out from bondage in Egypt.

Jesus -- God's son -- his life also became threatened. King Herod gave an order that all baby boys must be killed. Do you remember? King Herod wanted to make sure his throne would not get overthrown by this baby's divine birth.

*"Then when Herod saw that he had been tricked by the magi, he became very enraged, and sent and slew all the male children who were in Bethlehem and all its vicinity, from two years old and under, according to the time which he had determined from the magi*

*(Matthew 2:16, NASB)."*

Once again, in the midst of all the worldly craziness -- baby boys being murdered -- baby Jesus' life got safeguarded. God kept Jesus safe for he, the promised Messiah, would need to grow up and become our Savior and Lord, the one who died on the cross to save the world. His coming and the resurrection power of Jesus defeating the grave that Easter morning serves to paint a different story than what we might otherwise read. In his coming and exiting of earth Jesus became our beautiful Christmas Joy. He brought to us meaning-ful life -- new life and fullness of joy.

Though we do not always understand the timing of birthing, and though newness does not always come at the times we would perhaps orchestrate things if we had the choice, God's timing stands supreme. God brings on scene newness in ways that often requires laboring, much like we see in the case of the birthing of a baby. It may feel that all hell breaks out during such a birthing season in our lives -- in actuality it really does. Satan and the powers of darkness seeks to destroy and kill off everything that God births for the good. *"The thief comes only to steal and kill and destroy; I came that they may have life, and have it abundantly (John 10:10, NASB)."* Our enemy, the devil, wants nothing more than to destroy that which God births.

We rejoice when the labor pains cease and the delivery of a new baby comes at last. *"Whenever a woman is in labor she has pain, because her hour has come; but when she gives birth to the child, she no longer remembers the anguish because of the joy that a child has been born into the world (John 16:21, NASB)."* The new baby arrives, and now friends, family, and acquaintances come in party style, celebrating with the parents. The same can be said to an extent of spiritual birthing. God allows for us to take part in birthing something in a spiritual sense--a new ministry or a new book for example -- people do genuinely join us in celebrating.

Most do not realize all the behind the scenes laboring that has taken place to get to this point of spiritual delivery. Those around you do not know about the months of having this newness being carried inside of an impregnated womb. They do not understand all the laboring and pain endured. Additionally, the timing may have come at the same time as much enemy warfare -- remember the enemy does not want you to birth anything good. Rest assured, the people around you -- friends and mere acquaintances -- do not have to know all that. Rejoice in the newness that God has brought about in your life. Rejoice that he has chosen to do something new in you and through you. Rejoice in the fruit of your labor.

Your life has been changed, transformed even more through the process of what you have gone through. The baby has arrived (or maybe you might find yourself pregnant, still awaiting for delivery). Can you stand back for a moment and just take notice of how God provided and made such birthing possible? Christmas Joy has come! Christmas Joy has arrived! When we give birth in the spirit realm, we participate in such joy!

If you have given birth to something that God placed in you, then know this -- He still continues to work in your life. Just as in the physical sense, families continue growing with more and more babies being born, look out, be watchful; most likely you will once again become spiritually pregnant. Welcome to Christmas Joy! Welcome to intimacy with the Holy Spirit. Continue to make the choice to follow Jesus all the way and allow God to create and extend the Kingdom of God through you. You are alive in Christ. Continue multiplying and being fruitful. Continue allowing this Christmas Joy to reproduce in your life.

*"But God, being rich in mercy, because of His great love with which He loved us, even when we were dead in our transgressions, made us alive together with Christ (by grace you have been saved), and raised us up with Him, and seated us with Him in the heavenly places in Christ Jesus, so that in the ages to come He might show the surpassing riches of His grace in kindness toward us in Christ Jesus (Ephesians 2:4-7, NASB)."*

I have come to realize that just as in Mary's case, we get impregnated in the spirit by the Holy Spirit. He births dreams into reality. Visions become seeds to the birthing of new ideas, inventions, ministries, and more. Mary did not conceive Jesus by natural means, and neither do we bear God seeds in the natural. That does not mean that we do not have to exert any type of physical effort, quite the opposite. Sometimes the biggest dreams that the Holy Spirit births in us require a great deal of physical sacrifice to see them come to fruition.

*"Now the birth of Jesus Christ was as follows: when His mother Mary had been betrothed to Joseph, before they came together she was found to be with child by the Holy Spirit r(Matthew 1:18, NASB)."*

When we have the heart beat of God and become sensitive to His call, and as we then surrender our lives, our very beings become the temple of the Holy Spirit and God moves in us and through us to accomplish his good pleasure. *"for it is God who is at work in you, both to will and to work for His good pleasure (Philippians 2:13, NASB)."* As you reflect on the joyful birth of Jesus, take time to reflect on all the God seeds placed inside of you. Take time to not abandon your hopes and dreams --- just maybe they have been placed there by God. Your heart might just be housing God's heart desires and dreams to come to fruition in and through you. Get ready to birth your baby, God given, God breathed, and guarded!

## Just a Seed

Just a seed planted in love.
Just a seed poured down from above.
Go deep, go deep inside my heart.
Go deep, go deep inside my heart.
More than just an ordinary seed,
The King of kings came for me.
Seed of eternal Word plant in me
I receive. I receive such a
most magnificent Seed.

Sweet baby Jesus born that day so
long ago. God wrapped up so
tenderly in flesh all aglow. Sweet
baby Jesus born to die for me. Sweet
baby Jesus forever to You I sing.

May my heart hold Your Spirit so dear.
Fill my being with Your presence and let
Me know that You are here.

Let me live for you I plead.
No more fleshly, worldly ways,
No more hatred, no more shame.
Holy Spirit live in me.
Holy Spirit wash me clean.

## Birthing Prayer

Lord, thank you so much for caring so deeply for each of us. I pray right now for all those who read this book, Christmas Joy. You Lord, do birth babies in the physical sense and you also birth newness in each of us that receive your special gift of life.

Thank you for coming as a baby in a manger. Thank you for being clothed in flesh and humbling yourself in such a manner. Thank you for modeling for us how to live and how to love.

Continue placing your seeds, your Word in our hearts. Continue to birth your dreams and your heart beat in us. Let no thorns choke the seeds that you place inside of us. We receive your Word. We receive you. Continue all that you have started in us. Continue all that you have started in each person that reads Christmas Joy, and may the joy found in knowing you radiate in each of us this Christmas season and every day of our lives.

In Jesus name,

Amen

# Christmas Snow

*"Behold, I was brought forth in iniquity*
*And in sin my mother conceived me.*
*Behold, You desire truth in the innermost being,*
*And in the hidden part You will make me know wisdom*
*Purify me with hyssop, and I shall be clean;*
*Wash me, and I shall be whiter than snow.*
*(Psalm 51:5-7, NASB)."*

Snow covered mountain banks, tall trees planked with whiteness, and partaking of pure, clean ice cream -- clean, clean snow -- when I think of snow, I think of clean. Granted snow does not always appear that way, often dirt and mud get intertwined and a muddy slush oozes all around. However, when imagining Christmas snow, it must shine pure white for I relate it to the symbolism of washing away of sin and shame, the new life in Christ, that cleanliness that apart from Jesus would never come. Without the cross, without a Savior, without Resurrection Sunday, Jesus coming in the first place as that Christmas babe would have certainly held no meaning. I have heard it said that some believe that in order to really understand and be apart of God's unfailing purity and love, you must also dabble in the dark side -- the worldly side and experience both good and evil, both the white, clean side and the dark, black bleak side of life simultaneously. I want to extinguish this lie with no further consideration. Nothing can be further from the truth. Jesus came to bring hope to such a worldly and sinful state of existence.

He did not come to encourage it. *"You are the light of the world. A city set on a hill cannot be hidden (Matthew 5:24, ESV)."* Where you find light, darkness must flee -- when the Holy Spirit comes to richly dwell in you, then you no longer have any room for darkness to reside in you. No, you cannot clean yourself up by yourself, but God can. God can do it.

When someone goes out into the elements and gets filthy with dirt and grime, a shower or bath serves well to clean the body. In his Word, God calls us to apply the same principle to our inner being, our spiritual person. We come into the atmosphere of a secular world filled with much wickedness and pride. On a daily basis we need to repent from things we have done wrong -- that means we accept God's forgiveness and we turn away from those things and commit to walking through life differently -- apart from the evil nature. In explaining this Isaiah writes, *"'Come now, and let us reason together,' Says the Lord, 'Though your sins are as scarlet, They will be as white as snow; Though they are red like crimson, They will be like wool. (Isaiah 1:18, NASB).'"* No, this does not mean if you have brown skin, then all the sudden your skin turns white. I believe the picture becomes one of purity and wholeness -- only through Jesus can we truly become that clean.

Upon examining the context in which Isaiah penned the verse "'*Come now, and let us reason together... (Isaiah 1:18, NASB)*" we must take a step back and examine the verses or words proceeding this powerful statement of our sins being washed away -- white as snow. God expressed his displeasure in all the sacrifices of the people. They had been offering sacrifices for hundreds of years. This process of offering sacrifices had actually been put into place by God himself. At first glance, it could read a little confusing. Why would God who put the process of offering sacrifices in place now declare displeasure with the continuing of this act of service? I believe people's hearts had grown cold. They lived lives of sin and did not worship God fully. They were going through the motions of the law -- offering sacrifices.

They were not really understanding with their heart that God desires communion and intimacy with his people. Additionally, these animal sacrifices provided a temporary means of admitting faults and requesting the God of the universe to cleanse them. The animal sacrifices were not a perfect sacrifice. This ritual, repeated over and over again, and surely foreshadowed the perfect sacrifice provided --- Jesus.

When I think of the Christmas season, I do think of snow. In America, the Christmas season comes during our winter season, and many parts of our nation experience the coldness of snow falling. One reason I live in Southern California, but not in the mountains of our state has to do with the weather. It has only snowed possibly once at my home since coming here from Texas; however, even that one time may not have been snow as it looked more like sleet, and quickly melted away. For many living in America, snow invades their territories, their home, every winter. The blanket of white falling upon rooftops, hilltops, and river banks glistens and looks very beautiful.

"'I know your deeds, that you are neither cold nor hot; I wish that you were cold or hot. So because you are lukewarm, and neither hot nor cold, I will spit you out of My mouth. Because you say, 'I am rich, and have become wealthy, and have need of nothing,' and you do not know that you are wretched and miserable and poor and blind and naked, I advise you to buy from Me gold refined by fire so that you may become rich, and white garments so that you may clothe yourself, and that the shame of your nakedness will not be revealed; and eye salve to anoint your eyes so that you may see (Revelations 3:15-18, NASB)."*

Basically, the Bible conveys that it would have been better for us to not to have come to know God in the first place --- to have a coldness about our walk with him -- or to know him and walk him well --- to have a fiery relationship with him. He purifies and refines us in God's Kingdom -- the final state as expressed in Revelations, the last book of the Bible does not sound very good at all. "I will spit you out of My mouth." Listen, we have all been there -- we have just gone through the motions and "played" the part of believing in the baby Jesus of Christmas. Somehow, the warmth of love and intimacy for God may have gotten lost along the way. According to God's Word, that state of numbness leads to death -- it leads to being spit out of God's mouth. I pray that as you have been reading Christmas Joy, you have received a new spark or kindling of love inside of you. I pray that you reestablish, rekindle, reignite, and renew your relationship with the God who loves you so very much. If you have never entered into a close relationship with God in the first place, then I pray that you will embark on a close walk with him even from the start, and that the love you have will never grow old. May the Christmas Joy of Jesus come into your life in such a life changing and transforming way even this very day. Walking with God --- walking with the Holy Spirit inside -- absolutely, hands down has fulfillment and holds beauty like nothing else that you will ever experience.

Though Jesus came as our perfect sacrifice and died on the cross for us and rose again, our hearts still need activation. In our society, we too can just find ourselves going through the motions and not really loving God with our heart -- not loving God with our everything. We have heard the story of Jesus dying for us and that our sins are washed white as snow so much that perhaps it has become common place. I believe the Bible holds true. God would say to us "Come let us reason". Draw closer and step intimately into relationship with him. Jesus did not just come to wash us clean and remove sin from our lives, he came to draw us into an intimate daily relationship with him. When we consider the whiteness of Christmas snow step even more closely into such an intimate place knowing that you are loved more that you can possibly grasp.

In Isaiah we are encouraged *"Wash yourselves, make yourselves clean; Remove the evil of your deeds from My sight. Cease to do evil, Learn to do good; Seek justice, Reprove the ruthless, Defend the orphan, Plead for the widow (Isaiah 1:16-17, NASB)."* I believe God calls us to examine the root cause of the dirt and sin in our lives. We need to come with hearts of repentance and examination. Yes, grace certainly holds us; however, we continue to transform and throw off the things that hold us down -- we throw off sinful ways and follow in the truth of God.

We get blessed by God's grace and favor, by his forgiveness, by his love. We put on new life by stepping into Christ and then we get baptized. The Holy Spirit continues washing us every day. Much like in the natural sense we bathe daily, also we need to bathe in Living Water more than once -- daily we commune with God and allow the Holy Spirit to wash us as clean as pure snow -- no mud, no dirt, no impurities remain.

When I think of the Christmas season and the white, white snow, I also am reminded of snowmen. I am reminded how much fun everyone has getting out and playing in the snow, rolling hopefully large balls of snow and stacking them together. I think of the various ways people have creatively dressed up snowmen and even made it look like the snowmen had smiley faces and quite the personality.

Wow, so much fun! You too may have beautiful memories of snow and trying to build and decorate snowmen. What a great way to play and spend time in the winter. In some ways, many of us dress up like snowmen. I mean that metaphorically of course. We get ready to go out to events and nice places and get all dressed up and fix hair and all. I am not saying not to do that; I think that's actually nice. I enjoy dressing up for occasions as well. However, I wonder how many times we look all put together on the outside when in actuality on the inside our lives have some problem spots and need some extra TLC (Tender Loving Care). The rest of the world busily spinning around us see the makeup, the nice clothes, our stylishness, and think everything is fine. They think our life on the inside looks like what they see on the outside. I have bad news and some amazing good news for you! Again, we have all been there. We need to address the inside state of our inner being.

Jesus came to address that very thing. God sees all and knows all. He looks upon us in his amazing love. His desire though has beauty in the works. He does not just look on the outside, rather he clearly sees and knows everything about us and sees even on the inside. Yet, out of his love he has sent Jesus to make a way for us to step into his amazing plan of abundant life. The transformation in our lives does not come about on our own. The Holy Spirit coming to live inside of us makes such change. *"But we all, with unveiled face, beholding as in a mirror the glory of the Lord, are being transformed into the same image from glory to glory, just as from the Lord, the Spirit (2 Corinthians 3:18, NASB)."* Listen, I would not cut my own hair, it certainly would not come out right. Haircutting really does not fall into my talented zones. Similarly, the beautifying and purifying in my life comes from the workings of the Holy Spirit who lives in me.

This transformation does not come from me just wanting to be a "better person." It comes from entering into a relationship with God. It comes through accepting all Jesus did for me --- he came as that baby, he grew up to be the one that died on the cross to pay the price for the sin in my life. Keep diving into the Word of God and searching out the Scripture to see for yourself that what I am sharing with you has truth. Step into such truth and let God know you want to enter into that relationship with him. If you have not already received the Holy Spirit, this gift of God will come into you upon being baptized if it has not already. See Acts 2:38. *"Peter said to them, "Repent, and each of you be baptized in the name of Jesus Christ for the forgiveness of your sins; and you will receive the gift of the Holy Spirit." (Acts 2:38, NASB).* I recognize that the interpretation of this verse varies among believers. I believe we identify with the death and resurrection of Jesus when we respond in obedience and get baptized. I also do believe we receive the Holy Spirit into our lives as stated here. I encourage you to search the Scriptures out for yourself. In any case, please allow the very heart of the Bible, the love letter of God, the story of why Jesus came to earth in the first place gain your full attention and choose you this day to either walk away in total disbelief, or step in fully --- not just part way. You won't be disappointed when choosing to step fully in. Discover the joy of Christmas. Discover Jesus!

# Purify

Snow white and pure,
That's what I desire.
Wash me clean and
purify me.

Radiant and clean
May I be. On fire
And brightly shining,
Let my life be.

Come Holy Spirit,
Come Holy Spirit,
Come inside of me.

# Transforming Prayer

Dear Lord,

Thank you so much for all the transformation you do in lives this very day.

We cannot possibly clean ourselves by our own efforts and our own trying.

We thank you Holy Spirit for residing inside. Thank you for your transforming process that you do our lives. We welcome you and invite you today to continue that which you have begun.

In Jesus  name.

Amen

# Evergreen

"For God so loved the world, that He gave His only begotten Son, that whoever believes in Him shall not perish, but have eternal life (John 3:16, NASB)."

The most beautiful gift of all lasts forever and ever. As I begin to write this final chapter, the Holy Spirit whispers that this book will outlive me and that my grandkids will be reading the words that I am typing today. Oh, what a joy! Everlasting joy! As you have read the pages of this book, I hope you have encountered the best gift of all! I want you to know that Christmas Joy found in Jesus lasts forever. Oh, don't miss it! Please don't miss it! It outlast this body that clothes my inner me. Because of a baby that was not just any ordinary baby, I know I will see my grandkids if they too choose this everlasting treasure of Joy. So, shall we embark on this evergreen journey. Though this may look like the last chapter in this book, this one really does not end because of everlasting love much like an evergreen tree.

Evergreen trees have fascinated me so much. Unlike other trees, they keep their green leaves or pine needles through the seasons. When other trees have leaves that turn colors and then fall off, these evergreens endure the weathering of autumn and the coldest snowy winters. They endure even hot summer seasons and have even been known to withstand raging wild fires. Evergreen trees have become entwined in my mind and heart as a very intricate part of the Christmas season. As tears stream down my face as I type, I know my words may not as pristinely capture all that these evergreens have come to represent over the years to me. Let me begin by sharing about "evergreen" love.

An evergreen type of love last forever and ever. It never fails and it certainly never end. Christmas Joy has roots in this evergreen love. *"If I speak with the tongues of men and of angels, but do not have love, I have become a noisy gong or a clanging cymbal (1 Corinthians 13:1, NASB)."* We find this kind of love expressed in the Bible over and over again. No, we do not see it called "evergreen" love in the Bible; however, the evergreen trees remind me of this kind of lasting love. The love that God has towards you and me. It continues to radiate from heaven to earth year after year and touches all generations now and to come. We know love because of God's love towards man. *"The Lord is my shepherd, I shall not want. He makes me lie down in green pastures; He leads me beside quiet waters (Psalm 23:1-2, NASB)."* He constantly oozes out love and showers it upon us over and over again. I have no doubt that sending Jesus to earth as a baby greatly demonstrated such love. Why else would the God I know step down and become a baby who grew up into a man?

Yes, evergreen trees are fertile and produce "fruit" in season. For example, a pine tree produces pine cones -- healthy ones produce many.  In the Bible, we as followers of Christ want to live fruitful lives. We want to have a richness overflow from our lives, right? Such fruitfulness abounds as we understand our relationship with Jesus, this baby in the manger. As he walked among us here on earth, he put it this way. *"Abide in Me, and I in you. As the branch cannot bear fruit of itself unless it abides in the vine, so neither can you unless you abide in Me.  I am the vine, you are the branches; he who abides in Me and I in him, he bears much fruit, for apart from Me you can do nothing (John 15:4-5, NASB)."* Our sustenance for life and for bearing spiritual fruit like joy, peace, patience, kindness, and goodness (Galatians 5:22)--and for seeing those coming up after us coming to know and live out God's love story -- these all stem from spending time with God and seeing Jesus as our very source of life.  Our lives become like that evergreen tree. *"He will be like a tree  firmly planted by streams of water, Which yields its fruit in its season And its leaf does not wither; And in whatever he does, he prospers (Psalm 1:3, NASB)."*

Listen to this description of trees in God's Kingdom. *"On either side of the river was the tree of life, bearing twelve kinds of fruit, yielding its fruit every month; and the leaves of the tree were for the healing of the nations (Revelations 22:2, NASB)."* One day healing will come to the nations from the throne of God we know that healing will come as we read about the trees found there. When I see evergreen trees and think about their fruitfulness and that their leaves withstand and endure, it helps me to get a glimpse of the tree of life. The leaves of the tree of life drip with healing.

Do you want to know something crazy and amazing? God describes his followers as being like fruitful trees, and he also has blessed us with gifts. Leaves dripping with healing does not require waiting until we see with our physical eyes the throne of God. God's Holy Spirit flows through us and though Jesus no longer walks this earth and performs all those miracles that we read about in the Bible, our lives reflect his everlasting love and presence in us. The Holy Spirit lives in us and also touches other people that we meet. Healing represents one of the manifestations of the Holy Spirit in us. The more we get to know God, the more we get to know Jesus, the more we experience his presence and his power in our daily lives. We do not live lonely lives, rather we live in intimacy with God walking with us daily.

How do we enter into such a beautiful relationship with God? First, realize why Jesus came to earth. *"For God so loved the world, that He gave His only begotten Son, that whoever believes in Him shall not perish, but have eternal life (John 3:16, NASB)."* Next, I think it's helpful to hear what Peter had to say to the first church that met together after Jesus' resurrection and ascension into heaven. There happened quite a commotion, those who gathered together in that upper room, encountered the Holy Spirit, or rather the Holy Spirit came upon them all. They started speaking in different languages, and people that were visiting heard them speaking in their own language.

At first because of how all the followers of Jesus were overcome by the Holy Spirit, these on lookers thought the followers of *Jesus* were drunk, but Peter boldly shared about how the Holy Spirit came. He also shared that Jesus defeated death, hell, and the grave. This one Jesus, that these same people had crucified as they cried out days before, "crucify, crucify" -- he defeated death and he actually rose again, and resides alive in heaven as God. The people became alarmed as they comprehended that Jesus really did turn out to be who he said he was while living and walking among them. They wanted to make things right and asked Peter what they should do. Peter said to them, *"Repent, and each of you be baptized in the name of Jesus Christ for the forgiveness of your sins; and you will receive the gift of the Holy Spirit (Acts 2:38, NASB)."*

Peter's answer still holds true today. Understand that God's amazing love came to earth -- Jesus came and he died for all that you have done wrong -- all sin, all disobedience to God. You make the choice. You choose to follow God or to reject him all together. If you choose to believe that Jesus came and died as reported in the Bible, then the next step involves turning from trying to live life on your own means, change your thinking, change your behavior and turn away from any worldly lifestyle that held you in its grip -- you repent. Next, when you get baptized, the Bible states clearly that you do receive the Holy Spirit in your life. The Holy Spirit lives in you and guides you and you now walk and live daily as a spirit filled son or daughter of God. You choose.

It starts with a deep knowing that God sent Jesus just for you and for me. God sent Jesus to show us his amazing love. Apart from such love, and receiving it, because of our sin, our imperfect state, hell would await us. Instead we look forward to everlasting life, and evergreen kind of life because of the Joy that came and lay in a manger that Christmas day. "He *who trusts in his riches will fall, But the righteous will flourish like the green leaf (Proverbs 11:28, NASB)."*

# Your Love Reached Down

Love reached down in the form
of baby King.


Jesus, you are my King.

Jesus, you are my treasure.
Your love came down.

Your love came down.


Everlasting love how can it be?
Everlasting joy inside of me.
Everlasting truth that sets men free.
Resides here, resides here,
Amazingly living inside of  me.


Thank you for such an amazing love!
Thank you for becoming a beautiful seed.
Now living and breathing for all to see..


Jesus you are our everlasting King!

# Closing Prayer

Right now I pray for all those who will be reading Christmas Joy. By authority of the King, I order all hindrances of thought be broken, that they may truly see. Lord, release your love and joy and unlock now belief everlasting in all who read.  Lord help each one take that  next step of faith and grow closer to you this Christmas season or whenever they are  reading this book. I pray that the seeds sown through this book go deep into every heart. I pray that eyes and ears and hearts be open to receive your amazing gift of eternal life. Give each the boldness to repent and turn to you dearest Lord -- turn to you not for just a moment, but for the rest of life -- a daily walk with you. Help them identify with you through baptism and I know you never lie and that they will receive t h e  Holy Spirit into their lives. Thank you Lord for  all who have already believed and received. Help them to continue the journey forever with Thee.

In the amazing love of Jesus,
the one who came as the baby --
as Christmas Joy -- and grew up to be our King we now live!

We love You Jesus!
Amen.

Photo Credits to beautiful people who created the spectacular artwork for this book.

Africa Studio/Shutterstock.com

Alida Brivio/Shutterstock.com

Andreas Berheide/Shutterstock.com

Anelina/Shutterstock.com

Aquagreen Creative/Shutterstock.com

Astarina/Shutterstock.com

Bahtiar Maulanaa/Shutterstock.com

Cammep/Shutterstock.com

Christos Georghiou/Shutterstock.com

DenisProduction.com/Shutterstock.com

Derek Hatfield/Shutterstock.com

D-Krab/Shutterstock.com

Favore Studio/Shutterstock.com

Fotosvectores/Shutterstock.com

Gino Santa Maria/Shutterstock.com

Guschenkova/Shutterstock.com

Ianmitchinson/Shutterstock.com

Irena Peziene/Shutterstock.com

Jose AS Reyes/Shutterstock.com

Kaspars Grinvalds/Shutterstock.com

Kjpargeter/Shutterstock.com

Kovadenys/Shutterstock.com

Kuznetsov Alexey/Shutterstock.com

Liderina/Shutterstock.com

LightwaveMedia/Shutterstock.com

Lucky Business/Shutterstock.com

Maria Tiazhkun/Shutterstock.com

Mcchid04/Shutterstock.com

Myimagine/Shutterstock.com

Mythja/Shutterstock.com

Nardin29/Shutterstock.com

Nataleana/Shutterstock.com

Nazar Yosyfiv/Shutterstock.com

Novi Elysa/Shutterstock.com

Papkin/Shutterstock.com

PaulTarasenko/Shutterstock.com

Pavika Thummavuttikul/Shutterstock.com

RonTech3000/Shutterstock.com

Sidecoret/Shutterstock.com

SidorArt/Shutterstock.com

Standret/Shutterstock.com

Subbotina Anna/Shutterstock.com

Suzanne Tucker/Shutterstock.com

TitoOnz/Shutterstock.com

TTphoto/Shutterstock.com

Vasmila/Shutterstock.com

Verca/Shutterstock.com

Vicgmyr/Shutterstock.com

Victor Wong/Shutterstock.com

Volodymyr Tverdokhlib/Shutterstock.com

Yuganov Konstantin/Shutterstock.com

Zivica Kerkez/Shutterstock.com

## Amazing Christmas Joy!

The book has reached its end. However, your Christmas Joy has just barely started. Let the Christmas Joy found in Jesus be yours forever more.  Drop me a note. Make sure to put "Christmas Joy!" in the subject line. I look forward to hearing from you at Nancy@NBVelasco.Com

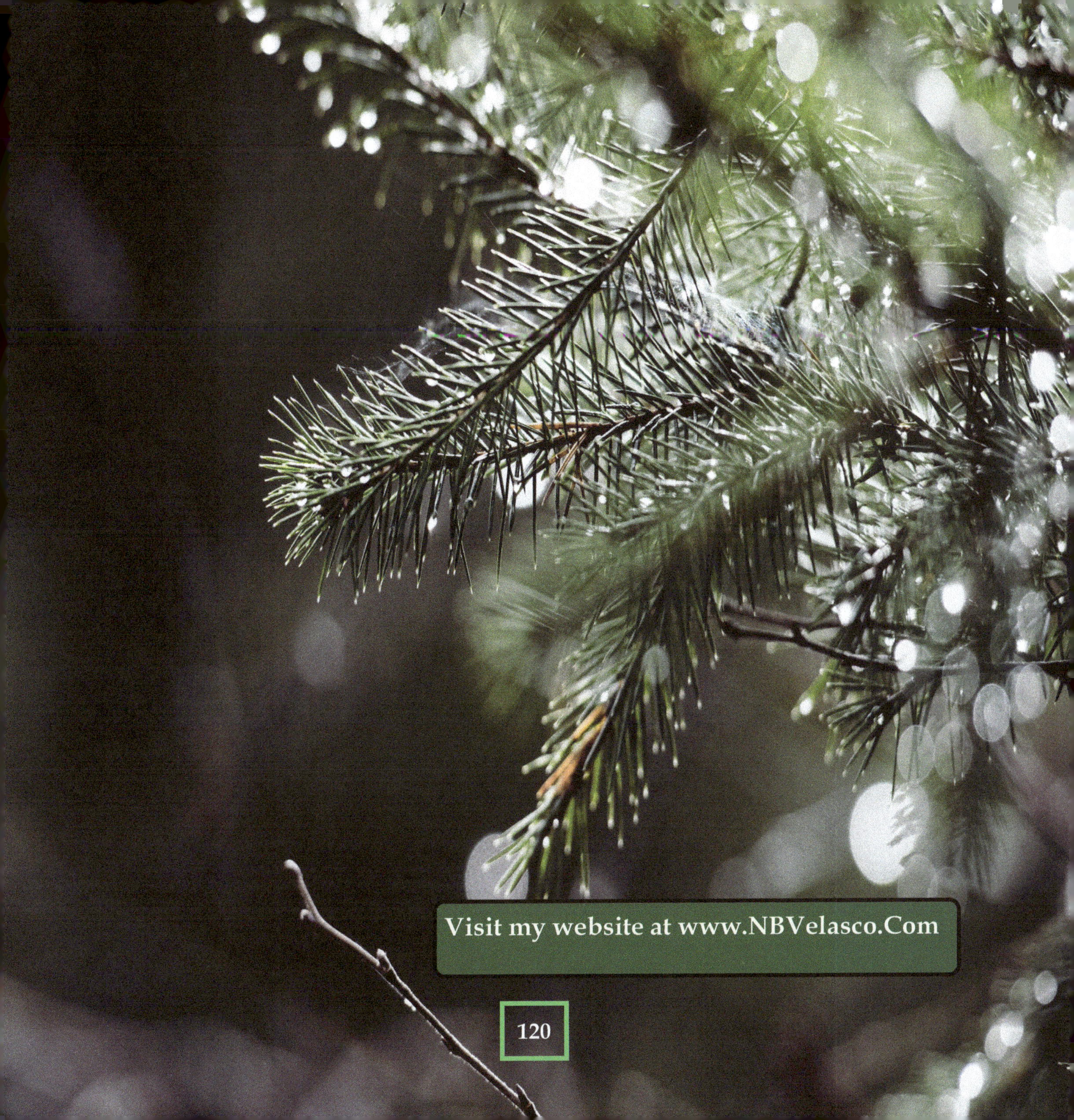

Visit my website at www.NBVelasco.Com

www.ingramcontent.com/pod-product-compliance
Lightning Source LLC
Chambersburg PA
CBHW040247100426

42811CB00011B/1177